The Astrology of
Haumea
Neptune's Higher Octave

Alan Clay
Melissa Billington

A Dwarf Planet University Publication

A Dwarf Planet University Publication
Copyright Alan Clay 2023

Artmedia
72 / 26 Antill St
Dickson ACT 2602
Australia
www.dwarfplanet.university
alan@artmedia.com.au

The Astrology of Haumea
Neptune's Higher Octave
ISBN: 978-0-6458033-1-0
ALL RIGHTS RESERVED

Cover image by astrologer, Karen La Puma
Author of the series, *A Toolkit for Awakening*
Karenlapuma.com

© 2023 All Rights Reserved – This work is copyright. Except for the purposes of fair reviewing, no part of this publication may be reproduced or transmitted in any form or by any means, without permission in writing from the publisher. The moral right of the authors has been asserted.

Contents

New Stars for a New Era **9**
Physical and Orbital **11**
Myth **14**
Sabian Symbol for the Discovery Degree . . **16**
Haumea as a Higher Octave **18**
    Higher Octave Case Study – *I have a Dream* 19
Discovery Events **23**
Astrological Meaning **25**
    Letting Go of the Old 27
Case Study – Diana, Princess of Wales . . . **28**
    Transit Case Study – Royal Wedding 30
    Transit Case Study – Royal Divorce 32
Case Study – Joseph Campbell **35**
    Transit Case Study - Hero with a Thousand Faces . . 38
Haumea in the Signs **40**
    Haumea in Leo 40
    Haumea in Virgo 41
    Haumea in Libra 41

Haumea in the Houses 43
    1st House 43
    2nd house 44
    3rd House 45
    4th house 46
    5th house 47
    6th House 48
    7th house 49
    8th house 50
    9th House 51
    11th House 53
    12th House 55

Workbook to Onboard Haumea 56

Haumea's Place in our New Firmament ... 58

Dwarf Planets as Higher Octaves 64

Dwarf Planet University 66
    Community Program 67
    What Students Say: 67

Meet the Writers 70

New Stars for a New Era

Many astrologers believe that new planets are discovered when we are ready to incorporate the new consciousness represented by that planet into our existing consciousness. We've noticed this with the discovery of Uranus, Neptune and Pluto over the last two hundred years, and now with the discovery of ten more planets we're entering a period of rapid consciousness development.

Our personal consciousness develops within the collective consciousness around us, and we see this personal consciousness mapped out in the personal planets in our chart. These are the planets out to Saturn that are visible to the naked eye, and they talk about facets of our personality that are important in living day to day.

When we are at personal planet consciousness, everything that is important is our feelings, our ideas and values, our agency and the luck and material rewards that brings us. "You can't take it with you, right?" And at this level we tend not to be conscious of the action of the outer planets our lives.

The inner planets represent aspects of personality, and the outer planets represent aspects of consciousness. So, as each outer planet is discovered, it represents a new aspect of consciousness that is coming available to us. The discovery of Uranus brought us intuitive consciousness, the discovery of Neptune, spiritual consciousness, and the discovery of Pluto, psychological consciousness.

So, the discovery of Haumea represents a new aspect of consciousness that is becoming available to us. Put simply Haumea takes the psychic opening of Neptune and turns it into real psychic connection with the oneness of our existence, with the magic of being alive. However, this new consciousness doesn't kick in automatically, rather we must actively incorporate it into our lives.

And because these outer planets talk of consciousness, how they manifest in our lives depends on our current level of consciousness. Most people on the planet experience the outer planets as unconscious influences, where these esoteric new energies are only perceived when, like Pluto, they barge into our lives in a confrontational way, because we haven't been sensitive and adaptable in the lead up.

As we develop spiritually, however, and consciously on-board these new energies into our lives, they become like guides into new territory, offering us special skills or challenges, depending on the aspects in our chart. At this level, rather than unconscious influences, the outer planets become like a new super-consciousness.

So, the discovery of so many new outer planets at one time represents a feast of new consciousness that is now available to us. The enlightenment that until now was only available to select gurus and priests is now available to everyone. But just like the gurus had to practice devoutly to be able to handle this divine power, we need to work to on-board these new energies consciously in our lives.

Physical and Orbital

One of the main ways we discern the meaning of new planets is to look at their physical and orbital characteristics. It tells us a lot about Saturn, that he has 82 moons, 150 moon-like objects, and rings. The precision required for that speaks of his structuring and limiting principals. Uranus spins with East West poles and rotates around the Sun in the opposite direction from most of the other planets, that's very bohemian.

Haumea is a dwarf planet located beyond the orbit of Neptune and Pluto, and she takes around 283 years to make a single orbit around the Sun. For her size Haumea is the most bizarrely shaped planet, more resembling an egg than a globe. She is the fastest rotating body in our solar system, so a day on Haumea is just under four hours long. Curiously, she rotates end on end, and this rotation is so fast it is near the point where a planet of this size starts to break down. If she were to rotate any more rapidly, she would distort into a dumbbell shape and split in two.

This unique shape, which looks like a rugby ball, suggests her energy is playful. And together with her fast rotation, it symbolizes a constant renewal and a joy in life. It also speaks of the day-to-day pressures we experience which might reshape us, and also of the danger that it might all spin out of control.

She is the fourth largest dwarf planet, and, like Saturn, she has a ring system. Rings connote limits and we know Saturn can be a limiting principle in our lives. So, these rings tell us that Haumea will also talk about limits. She has a large red spot which suggests the renewal of bloodlines, and the primal connection to embodiment that this goddess of birth and rebirth exemplifies as we shall see in the myth.

Haumea is the largest member of a family of objects with similar physical and orbital characteristics, which are thought to have formed when a larger progenitor was shattered by an impact. So, Haumea talks about being part of a family born of a collision with reality and teaches us the value of nurturing the disparate aspects of our psychic identity.

This family is the first to be identified in our solar system, and they are thought to have migrated to their current orbit from the outer reaches, which is the Scattered Disc. So, in today's world where many of us are seeking a sense of belonging, of connection to land or place, Haumea also talks about migration to a new home. We have increased levels of migration from political persecution and accelerating global climate change and Haumea is here to remind us of what joins us together.

Most of her surface appears to be pure crystalline water ice which makes her appear as bright as snow. This is peculiar because the temperature in these outer reaches should be too cold for this type of ice, which should also be coloured by the sun's radiation. This suggests that Haumea and her family members have undergone recent resurfacing that produced fresh ice. So, she is linked with life through the water on her surface, and she talks about a process of renewal.

Notably she is in a 7:12 orbital resonance with Neptune, which means that she does 7 revolutions around the Sun for every 12 of Neptune's. This gravitational resonance between their cycles links her with Neptune's spiritual nature, and, like a transformer, raises his spirituality to a higher level.

Where with Neptune's belief there is often a question of faith, Haumea steps that up so there is no question. For her spirituality is inherent in the embodied experience. It transcends the dualistic mind of black or white, right or wrong, belief or non-belief. We simply know in our bones that we are interconnected.

Myth

The myth behind the name of these new planets also tells us a lot about their astrological meaning. Myths transmit knowledge across time and culture, but they need interpretation for the new time and the new culture.

Haumea is the guardian goddess of the island of Hawaii and the mother of volcano goddess Pele and her brothers and sisters. The islands of Hawaii are borne of volcanic activity, of molten lava explosively emerging out of the ocean. So, Haumea's regenerative effect in our lives can sometimes feel existential and hard to handle.

She is both a fire goddess and an earth goddess. So her power is a marriage of the explosive fire energy with the nurturing earth energy, an alchemy that is required to magically manifest new life.

In the Hawaiian creation myth Haumea gave birth to many children from different parts of her body. With the help of a magic stick called the Makalei, she was renewed as a young woman several times, marrying her son and grandson each time, constantly growing old and being reborn. So, she is the planet of rebirth. Life is a process for Haumea, a process of rejuvenation.

She has a magical ability that enables her to ensure a never-ending food supply. Her magic stick also attracts fish and is associated with a tree of eternal bounty, so she works at a spiritual level to nourish and replenish our lives.

Myths told about her centre around themes of food, marriage, and birth. In one of these she transforms herself into a living tree in order to conceal her husband from those who want to sacrifice him. So, she represents a psychic shift from the world view that separates us from Nature to the embodied recognition and power of being one with Nature. When we connect with our psychic centre, we are able to protect those we love. Her love is all-encompassing and unconditional, but to enable this we have to leave our ego at the door.

In myth she gave humans the ability to give birth naturally. In another story she visited the daughter of a chieftain who was experiencing painful childbirth and discovered that humans only gave birth by cutting open the mother. Seeing this, she created a potion which allowed the mother to birth the baby naturally. As a reward she received "the tree of changing leaves" out of which gods are made.

It is significant that this planet has been discovered in a period when we see the increased prevalence of cesarian births across the globe. She reminds us that we have the power to create and regenerate our lives when we align with the natural world and its rhythms. As we embrace her energy, we embody the divinity in each moment. Creativity is inherent in her energy and the word *create* originates from the word *arise*. The fires of life arise slowly in the living plants that feed us, and also explode in fiery display out of the earth's volcanoes.

Sabian Symbol for the Discovery Degree

The Sabian Symbols were channelled by clairvoyant Elsie Wheeler and astrologer Marc Edmund Jones, and they give us rich visual symbols for each degree of the zodiac. The discovery degree of these new dwarf planets is like a birth moment as they arrive in our consciousness and the Sabian Symbol for that degree gives us another pathway to interpret this new astrological goddess.

Haumea was discovered at 13 degrees Libra and the Sabian Symbol for that degree is *Children Blowing Soap Bubbles*. Here is how this image has been interpreted by Marc and other key astrologers.

> *The keyword is enchantment. When positive, the degree is a consistent simplicity of character which enables anyone to maintain his touch with a transcendental magic of being, and when negative, a constant and idle daydreaming.*[1]

Marc Edmund Jones

> *This seems to refer to the use of the imagination and the value of fantasy in a collective setup. Men dream together as a preparation for acting together. Rituals related to the great aspirations of mankind are both*

---

[1] https://sabiansymbologist.wordpress.com/2022/10/03/libra-13-children-blowing-soap-bubbles-2/

sacred ceremonies and playthings for young minds; and so are court ceremonies and operas for the social elite, or baseball games for the crowds.[2]

Dane Rudhyar

Play is sometimes meaningless and yet very important to development. This symbol suggests there needs to be a light-hearted attitude in addition to the deep and meaningful, for it will be in fleeting moments of fun that pleasure, joy and companionship is found.[3]

Lynda Hill

So, this discovery symbol tells us that we can best access Haumea's deep spirituality through a spirit of play. Haumea brings us into touch with the magic of each moment, with the enchantment of being alive. This symbol reminds us to retain our light-hearted joy as the best way to connect with the divine, with the psychic oneness of humanity.

---

2   http://www.mindfire.ca/An%20Astrological%20Mandala/An%20Astrological%20Mandala%20-%20Libra%201-15.htm
3   https://sabiansymbols.com/symbols/

Haumea as a Higher Octave

A higher octave expresses an inner planet energy at a more spiritual level, and this gives us another way of understanding the new outer planets. We can think of the higher octave as the antidote to the small-mindedness of the inner planet energy, providing a way to elevate those qualities.

Traditionally Neptune is thought of as the higher octave of Venus, where her love of beauty and values is reflected in a more collective spiritual way with Neptune. And the spirituality of Neptune, in turn, provides an antidote to the sometimes-indulgent personal values of Venus by expanding our value system to include the collective.

We know that Haumea's orbit is in gravitational resonance with Neptune's, so we can look at Haumea as the higher octave of Neptune, stepping up his psychic opening into a real psychic connection with the collective consciousness. This connection anchors us and gives us support that counter-balances Neptune's nebulousness.

We see a love of beauty and of values in each of these planets, expressed in the personal realm by Venus, at a more spiritual level by Neptune, and on an even more esoteric level by Haumea.

Transpersonal astrologer Dane Rudhyar tells us that the higher octaves act on the lower octaves to repolarize them. Neptune acts on Venus, and in turn Haumea acts on Neptune. So, the regeneration of transpersonal Haumea can enliven the personal Venus expression of values and love, thus anchoring the unity consciousness of Haumea into the reality of day to day existence.

Higher Octave Case Study – *I have a Dream*

If these planets are higher octaves of one another, we would expect to see them singing in chorus at key moments in our lives. So, let's see if we can find Haumea, Neptune, and Venus singing in chorus in Martin Luther King's chart on the day he gave the 'I have a dream' speech, August 28th, 1963.

Natally, King has Venus in the 11th house of collective consciousness, in a wide opposition to Neptune in the 5th house of creativity, which is in a close semi-sextile with Haumea in the 4th house of home, so the three octaves are actively aligned in his chart. On the day of the speech, Venus and Haumea were conjunct in the sky, with both conjunct his natal Neptune within two degrees. So, we do see the higher octave resonance right there.

In the chart of a spiritually evolved person like King, the quintiles (72 degrees) represent evolutionary flow, and on the day his landmark speech transiting Neptune was quintile his natal Neptune, showing the evolutionary spiritual opportunity of the moment. And it was also quintile his Sun in the 9th house of belief, showing that he was the man of that moment.

Transiting Neptune was also sesquiquadrate Varuna, the higher octave of Saturn, on his 12th house cusp. While Saturn is all about control, structure, and limitation, Varuna rules simply through claiming sovereignty without the need to control. King was claiming his sovereignty through his actions on that day. And the placement on the cusp of the 12th allowed him to connect with the collective unconscious, so this speech has become an iconic turning point in the fight for black sovereignty.

20

Transiting Neptune was also in a stressful opposition to his Ascendant and square his natal Mercury in the 10th house of society, referencing the crisis of oppression that he was addressing in his speech.

And lastly, transiting Neptune was also sextile Quaoar in his 5th house of love and creativity. Quaoar is the planet of 'new perspectives', which we can think of as the higher octave of Jupiter. Quaoar is our first non-gendered planet, a supreme god of the Tongva, the indigenous people of what is now known as Los Angeles. Quaoar sings and dances a new reality out of the chaos of existence. In his speech King is 'singing and dancing' a dream of a new reality based on love.

Meanwhile, transiting Mercury in the sixth house of service was sextile King's natal Haumea in the 4th, and semi-sextile his natal Neptune in the 5th, drawing on both the higher octaves of Venus for his speech.

And Sedna, who represents our 'soul's path of destiny' in this life, was transiting in a supportive trine with Neptune, so King was fulfilling his spiritual destiny with his visionary words. Sedna was also in a demanding square with Haumea, indicating the long spiritual road ahead to achieve that dream. In the challenging environment of those holding on to old traditions, he was sowing the seeds of renewal for his people.

Transiting Haumea was strongly activating his birth chart. As well as conjoining Neptune, she was also semi-sextile her natal position, trine Jupiter in the 12th house of the collective unconscious and quintile Mars in the 2nd. And she was also inconjunct Uranus in the 12th and semi-square Pluto in the 3rd house of ideas and communication. These aspects speak of a rebirth (Haumea) which is centered in a dream (Neptune) and of a stressful relationship with power (semi-square Pluto) that would expand (Jupiter) in the collective unconscious (12th) through his evolutionary actions (quintile Mars) in the material world (2nd).

Remember transiting Venus and transiting Haumea were conjunct in the sky, so Venus reinforces this narrative with the same aspects, but also adds an evolutionary biquintile with his MC, so he was in the right place at the right time.

Transiting Eris, the higher octave of Pluto, in the 12th was closely semi-sextile his natal Venus in the 11th. Eris is a truth teller and in the 12th house she promotes deep spiritual truths. And transiting Varuna quintiles his Venus, which brought his sovereignty into an evolutionary flow with his values and lifted him into a genuine notability.

According to U.S. Representative John Lewis, who also spoke that day:

> *"Dr King had the power, the ability, and the capacity to transform those steps on the Lincoln Memorial into a monumental area that will forever be recognized. By speaking the way he did, he educated, he inspired, he informed not just the people there, but people throughout America and unborn generations."*[4]

Here we see the three octaves expressed: the education with Venus at the personal level, the inspiration of Neptune at the social and spiritual levels, and the 'reaching out to unborn generations' by the goddess of rebirth, Haumea, at an even more spiritual level.

---

4   https://en.wikipedia.org/wiki/I_Have_a_Dream

Discovery Events

Another way we can infer the meaning of new planets is to look at discovery events. These are events around the time of the Haumea's discovery which give us an understanding of the astrological energy of the planet. Haumea was discovered on 28 December 2004, and she can be linked to three discovery events.

Most astrologers link her with a major earthquake in the Indian Ocean which happened two days before she was discovered. This resulted in a tsunami which killed more people than any other tsunami in recorded history. We naturally think of this as a disaster, but the disaster came through our insensitivity to the world we live in. The animals on the other hand perceived the earthquake's initial rumblings, so they ran inland and virtually all of them survived.

When we're at the unconscious level and not tuned into the rumblings of the psychic unity, we experience Haumea's rebirth energy as disaster. At this level we are victims to circumstances we're not paying attention to. As we develop spiritually, we realize that there is no separation, that we are nature. And we learn to tune in to the power the earth offers and to the psychic energies around and within us which are constantly enriching our lives with knowledge.

Haumea brings new growth into our lives, but we must allow this process. We tend to hold onto the old because it gives us security, and if we do the new reality is born through disaster and crisis, rather than acceptance. Death and rebirth is a natural process and we have to surrender to this process, allowing the old to pass away and welcoming and trusting in what will emerge.

The second discovery event occurred the day before Haumea was discovered. This was the brightest extrasolar event known to humans and the strongest high-energetic gamma radiation burst measured so far on the planet. Extrasolar means that the energy didn't come from our sun but, in this case, from something called a magnetar! This is a type of neutron star with a powerful magnetic field, which is 10-25 times the mass of our sun.

This suggests that Haumea gives us a way to tune into the powerful energies around us and reinforces her psychic connection with the oneness of humanity. When we open ourselves to the energies around us, we will be nourished and energized by them, even when they are disruptive to our current status quo. But like the yogis of old we need to prepare our consciousness to receive this regenerative power, so we don't become overwhelmed or burnt out.

The third discovery event we link with Haumea is the development in 2004 of semantic social networks. These combine the connections between people, with the content produced or shared in their network. Through these networks it is possible to reclaim the intelligence of living beings and systems by paying attention to what's already happening.

Each thing that we want or need or can contribute, is interconnected with everyone else's wants, needs, and contributions. And when we're in touch with this psychic unity we can harvest collective intelligence. We make this connection with the oneness of humanity when we honour the expertise that we each bring to the equation.

Astrological Meaning

Haumea connects us to the psychic unity that exists across space and time, with the oneness of each of our existences, and she does this in each moment simply through the magic of being alive. She encourages us to live in the present and to savour every moment of life, allowing us to appreciate the beauty of the world around us, and within us.

Neptune's psychic opening has the potential to blossom into real psychic connection with Haumea, a connection to the soul level. We often understand soul on the individual level, yet when we have evolved and embraced Haumea in our lives, the soul level includes not only all of humanity but all beings. We are all one.

Haumea is always encouraging rebirth in our lives. She does this by encouraging a spirit of play within the sacred work we are doing. Play requires trust in the bigger picture. We need to allow ourselves to let go and explore the myriad of creative possibilities without judgment and that way we deepen the sacred.

However, when we experience Haumea's psychic connection unconsciously it can come with a righteousness similar to Neptune, but with a lot more psychic force behind it. As a result, we may ride roughshod over everyone, or stick our neck out about something and so we get ourselves into trouble.

Or, even more likely, we find no connection to the psychic source, so our life shrivels up and we live in a sort of spiritual starvation, a starvation of life energy. At the unconscious level we are likely to try and fill this lack of meaningful connection by indulging in the hollow pleasures of consumer society. But no amount of money can buy the connection we seek, so this just leaves us feeling even more alienated.

At this level we may respond by being overly dramatic and attention seeking, or by making claims of martyrdom. We become so desperate for meaningful connection that we will go to any lengths to achieve it. And there is also a danger our drama could spin out of control and bring everything in our lives crashing down.

As we develop a more spiritual approach, we learn to trust in the life process and deepen our connection to the psyche through allowing the magic-of-being in each moment. We all know those special moments when we are out in nature, or in the arms of our love, or deep in meditation, where we feel the lifeforce chorusing through us. This psychic connection to the oneness-of-life is the magic that Haumea opens us to in each moment.

There are times with Haumea that we might pick up too much psychic energy and need to withdraw, absorb, and refresh through rest, meditation, or sleep. With awareness and application, we can learn to offload the non-nutritive more readily and connect with a never-failing source of psychic sustenance.

Haumea throws us into experiences where we collide with consensus reality, but in that collision, we find a like-hearted community. This new family will be affected not only by our collisional arrival, but also by their own collision with reality. In these situations, we experience our shared interests, which creates a sense of family that transcends biology.

At the spiritual level she encourages us to find our community, to connect with a family of souls who can play important roles in our lives and to find a new way of living together with them. These people may be spread across the planet and may not be the obvious choice, but our connection with them will psychically nourish us and them.

And as we deepen this contact to source, we learn to facilitate a constant renewal in our own lives and in other's lives. We learn to ride the psychic waves and the lava flows that arise in each moment and to be accepting and creative with those opportunities. At this level we understand that the bountiful universe manifests through us when we are open to it. And, to enable this, we know that we have to leave our ego at the door and trust in the divine process.

Letting Go of the Old

Haumea is always bringing a renewal into our lives, but we have to welcome this and gracefully surrender the old, so there is space for the new to grow. However, our sense of security often derives from the possessions and routines that we have built up over many years and, as a result, we can become very attached to the old.

When we are rooted in the old for our security, we protect ourselves from any regeneration because we fear it will challenge the foundations of our world. But regeneration is essential for a healthy life: no living thing can maintain a stasis without growth. So, we have to be open to the growth, welcome it and nurture it.

When we hang on blindly to the old, the only way the new can be birthed is through crisis and disaster. By desperately hanging onto the old we are actually calling crisis and disaster into our lives to help us let go and allow the necessary rebirth.

Case Study – Diana, Princess of Wales

In myth, Haumea married her son and grandson, growing old each time and being renewed as a young woman. We see this same motif echoed in Diana's heritage. She was the daughter of the 8th Earl of Spencer with excellent lineage dating back to the 15th century, and wife of her 11th cousin once removed, Prince Charles, heir to the British throne.

Diana has Haumea in the 8th house at 0.15 Virgo. This first-degree placement is significant because it represents a new journey in this earth sign. It is less established in the energies of the sign but more in touch with the newness, the magic of being. In Virgo this manifests as the health of the body and in the 8th house that extends to the health of the collective energies.

What makes this placement on the cusp so strong is the conjunction with the North Node at 28.10 Leo and Mars at 1.39 Virgo. This gives her the ability to act, using the rejuvenating power of Haumea to fulfill her destiny, and then put it into action in the world. This powerful conjunction is in the 8th house of collective resources and deeper spiritual meaning, and she played a regenerative role not only in British society but across the globe with her charity work.

Haumea is sextile Mercury in the 7th, and she was a huge inspiration to many people for her charity work and became known for shifting social attitudes towards AIDS patients, as well as for her campaign for the removal of landmines. She was also a strong advocate for helping people with cancer and mental illness. This is her Haumea conjunct Mars in the 8th house of collective resources, as she worked to enact a rebirth

Name: ♀ Princess of Wales Diana [Adb]		
born on Sa., 1 July 1961	Time: 7:45 p.m.	ASTRO DIENST www.astro.com
in Sandringham, ENG (UK)	Univ.Time: 18:45	
0e30, 52n50	Sid. Time: 13:25:18	Type: 2.GW 0.0-1 6-Mai-2023

Natal Chart (Method: Web Style / Placidus)
Sun sign: Cancer
Ascendant: Sagittarius

☉ Sun	9 Can 39'47"		
☽ Moon	25 Aqu 2'17"		
☿ Mercury	3 Can 12' 5"r		
♀ Venus	24 Tau 23'59"		
♂ Mars	1 Vir 38'45"		
♃ Jupiter	5 Aqu 5'50"r		
♄ Saturn	27 Cap 48'50"r		
♅ Uranus	23 Leo 20'10"		
♆ Neptune	8 Sco 38'12"r		
♇ Pluto	6 Vir 2'39"		
☊ True Node	28 Leo 10'30"		
☋ Desc.T.Node	28 Aqu 10'30"		
⚷ Chiron	6 Pis 28' 5"r		
⊕ P.Fort.	3 Leo 47' 0"		
⚳ Ceres	10 Tau 37'36"		
136108 Haumea	0 Vir 14'34"		
136472 Makemake	3 Leo 14'16"		
225088 Gonggong	13 Aqu 13'32"r		
120347 Salacia	16 Cap 40'39"r		
136199 Eris	10 Ari 33'58"		
28978 Ixion	24 Lib 27'27"r		
90482 Orcus	9 Can 17'34"		
50000 Quaoar	18 Lib 38' 8"r		
90377 Sedna	28 Ari 19'43"		
20000 Varuna	19 Tau 10'47"		
AC: 18 Sag 24'31"	2: 29 Cap 48'	3: 18 Pis 21'	
MC: 23 Lib 3' 8"	11: 16 Sco 3'	12: 3 Sag 18'	

	C	F	M
F	ErSe	♅ ☊ ⊕ MaAC	
A	IxQuMC	☽ ♃ ☋ Go	
E	♄ Sa	♀ ⚳ Va	♂ ♇ Ha
W	☉ ☿ Or	♆	⚷

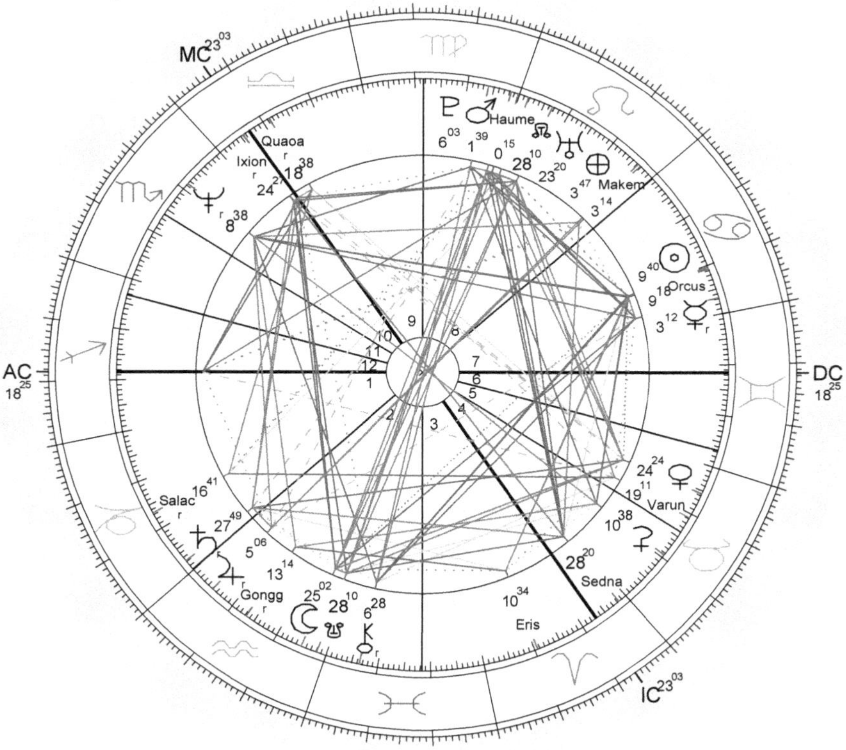

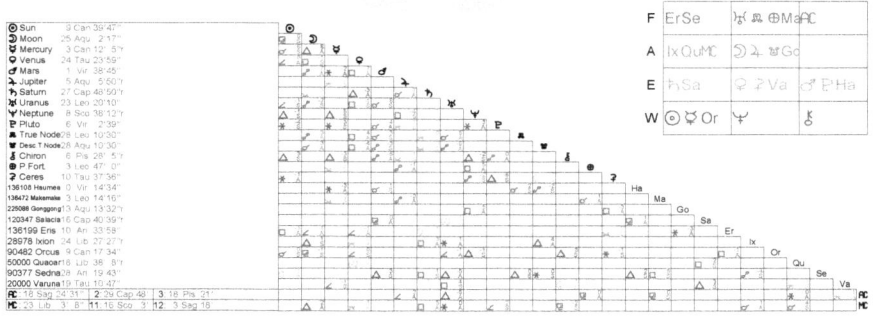

in the collective use of our energies.

Haumea is also opposite the Moon conjunct the South Node in her 2nd house, and she was plagued by emotional problems, in contrast to the public image she was required to uphold. Haumea is also trine Sedna in the 4th. Sedna connects us with our heritage, with the big lessons that our soul really wants to learn in this life. The 4th house Sedna is about family and ancestry, and we know she is the descendant of a long line of royal heritage. She brought the royal family into the modern world, and her children continue to do so.

Transit Case Study – Royal Wedding

She married in St. Paul's Cathedral on July 29, 1981, in a globally televised ceremony which was watched by an audience numbering in the hundreds of millions. She was adored.

On this day, Diana had transiting Ceres exactly conjunct natal Haumea, and Ceres is the give and take of love that keeps us alive. So, this transit indicates that her marriage opened the psychic flow of unconditional love that Haumea represents in her chart.

Transiting Eris was in the 3rd house and sesquiquadrate Haumea in the 8th, which speaks to the challenge that her entry into the royal family presented to the tradition. She wanted to be included but had to fit in to the strict protocols of being a royal family member. This challenge was manifested right at the start.

Transiting Quaoar in the 10th house was quintile Haumea. The quintile is an evolutionary opportunity, and in this house, Quaoar is about finding a social practice. So, by marrying a prince she took on the social practice of being a princess.

Transiting Haumea is on the cusp of the 9th house, in a close semisquare to her natal Makemake and Part of Fortune,

Name: ♀ Princess of Wales Diana [Adb]
born on Sa., 1 July 1961
in Sandringham, ENG (UK)
0e30, 52n50

Time: 7:45 p.m.
Univ.Time: 18:45
Sid. Time: 13:25:18

ASTRO DIENST
www.astro.com
Type: 2.GW 0.0-1 6-Mai-2023

Natal Chart (Method: Web Style / Placidus)
Sun sign: Cancer
Ascendant: Sagittarius
Transits 29 July 1981

31

which are exactly conjunct in the 8th house. The marriage challenged her to see herself in a bigger way. To step out from the background on issues of collective resources and collective energies, as she did with her charity work.

Haumea is also biquintile her natal Gonggong in the 2nd house. She was thrown in the deep end through this biquintile. Gonggong is a water god of flow and overflow, and she has him in the 2nd house. So, her high level of sensitivity necessitated boundaries, particularly with the royal family, and we see this dynamic right from the beginning. This aspect is also talking about the millions that adored her. Her level of empathy brought love out in others.

And transiting Haumea is also semi-sextile her natal Quaoar in the 9th house and square the Ascendant. Quaoar in the 9th house is about embodying spirit in our beliefs. Where the biquintile to Gonggong was talking about throwing her in the deep end, this transit is encouraging her to jump in and find her own playful way to revolutionize the conservative traditions. Because transiting Haumea was square the Ascendant, this task was not an easy one.

Finally, Haumea is trine her natal Varuna in the 5th house of love and passion. Varuna talks about our sovereignty and through this marriage she became a sovereign.

Transit Case Study – Royal Divorce

As a fairy-tale princess, we would expect her to live happily ever after, however the royal couple's divorce became final on August 28, 1996.

On that day transiting Saturn in her 3rd house was biquintile Diana's Haumea in the 8th house, the house of the deals we do in our marriage and of joint resources. The biquintile tells us that it was very good for her to have that divorce,

Name: ♀ Princess of Wales Diana [Adb] born on Sa., 1 July 1961 in Sandringham, ENG (UK) 0e30, 52n50	Time: 7:45 p.m. Univ.Time: 18:45 Sid. Time: 13:25:18	ASTRO DIENST www.astro.com Type: 2.GW 0.0-1 6-Mai-2023

Natal Chart (Method: Web Style / Placidus)
Sun sign: Cancer
Ascendant: Sagittarius
Transits 28 Aug. 1996

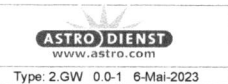

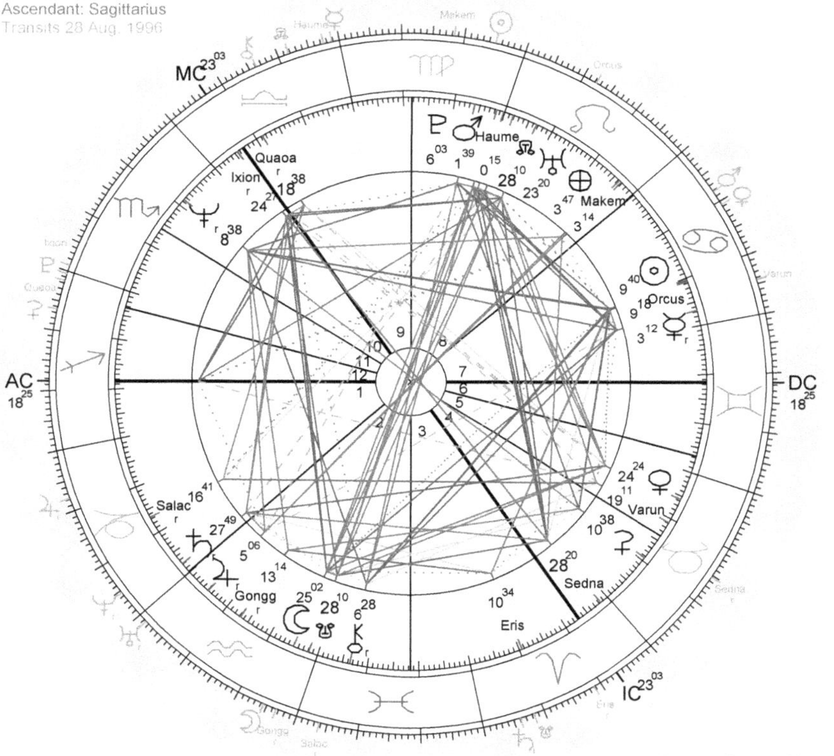

	C	F	M
F	ErSe	♅ ☊ ⊕ MaAC	
A	IxQuMC	☽ ♃ ☋ Gc	
E	♄Sa	♀ ⚳ Va	♂ ♇ Ha
W	☉ ☿ Or	♆	⚷

Natal				
☉ Sun	9 Can 39'47"			
☽ Moon	25 Aqu 2'17"			
☿ Mercury	3 Can 12' 5"r			
♀ Venus	24 Tau 23'59"			
♂ Mars	1 Vir 38'45"			
♃ Jupiter	5 Aqu 5'50"r			
♄ Saturn	27 Cap 48'50"r			
♅ Uranus	23 Leo 20'10"			
♆ Neptune	6 Sco 38'12"r			
♇ Pluto	6 Vir 2'39"			
☊ True Node	28 Leo 10'30"			
☋ Desc.T.Node	28 Aqu 10'30"			
⚷ Chiron	6 Pis 28' 5"r			
⊕ P.Fort.	3 Leo 47' 0"			
⚳ Ceres	10 Tau 37'36"			
136108 Haumea	0 Vir 14'34"			
136472 Makemake	3 Leo 14'16"			
225088 Gonggong	13 Aqu 13'32"r			
120347 Salacia	16 Cap 40'39"r			
136199 Eris	10 Ari 33'58"			
28978 Ixion	24 Lib 27'27"r			
90482 Orcus	9 Can 17'34"			
50000 Quaoar	18 Lib 38' 8"r			
90377 Sedna	28 Ari 19'43"			
20000 Varuna	19 Tau 10'47"			
AC: 18 Sag 24'31"	2: 29 Cap 48'	3: 18 Pis 21'		
MC: 23 Lib 3' 8"	11: 16 Sco 3'	12: 3 Sag 18'		

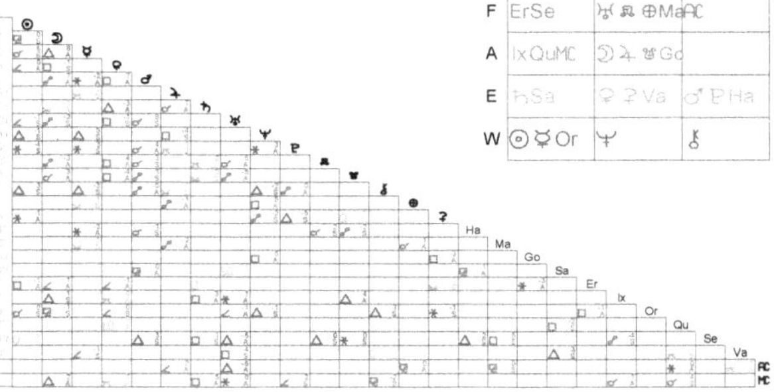

that it was an evolutionary opportunity. She didn't stop doing her public work, in fact she was freed to do her work. However transiting Pluto in the 11th house was square her natal Haumea, so the transformation wasn't easy. It was a challenge, but an important liberation for her.

Inevitably, because it was her divorce, transiting Haumea in her 9th house was squaring her Mercury that day, challenging her to think and communicate in new ways. However, Haumea was also sextile to her natal Makemake in the 8th house. Makemake talks about the nation, about the bigger context, and the sextile on her divorce lifted her role in the nation rather than ending it. She started touring the world and her charity work flourished. And transiting Haumea was also semi-sextile her Mars, freeing her to put her global connection with humanity into action.

Case Study – Joseph Campbell

Joseph Campbell was an American writer and leading authority and lecturer on mythology, the psyche, and symbolism. His book *Hero with a Thousand Faces* talks of the psychic unity in myth across all cultures.

Natally, he has Haumea closely conjunct Neptune in the 9th House. This means the two upper octaves of Venus are conjunct in the house of belief in his birth chart. He was a professor of comparative mythology, and his theory sees all mythic narratives as variations of a single great story. The theory is based on the observation that a common pattern exists beneath the narrative elements of most great myths, regardless of their origin or time of creation. The central pattern most studied by Campbell is often referred to as the hero's journey and was first described in his book *The Hero with a Thousand Faces.*

His Haumea/Neptune conjunction is closely semi-sextile his Moon in the 10th house. His ideas regarding myth and its relation to the human psyche are dependent on the work of Jung, whose studies of human psychology greatly influenced Campbell. His conception of myth is closely related to the Jungian method of dream interpretation, which is reliant on symbol interpretation. And Jung's insights into archetypes were heavily influenced by *The Tibetan Book of the Dead*.

Campbell's Haumea/Neptune conjunction is closely sesquiquadrate his Saturn in the 4th house of sacred ground. He often described mythology as having a fourfold function within human society.

Name: ♂ Joseph Campbell [Adb]			ASTRO DIENST www.astro.com
born on Sa., 26 March 1904	Time:	7:25 p.m.	
in New York, NY (US)	Univ.Time:	0:25 27 Mar.	
74w00, 40n43	Sid. Time:	7:45:03	Type: 2.GW 0.0-1 6-Mai-2023

Natal Chart (Method: Web Style / Placidus)
Sun sign: Aries
Ascendant: Libra

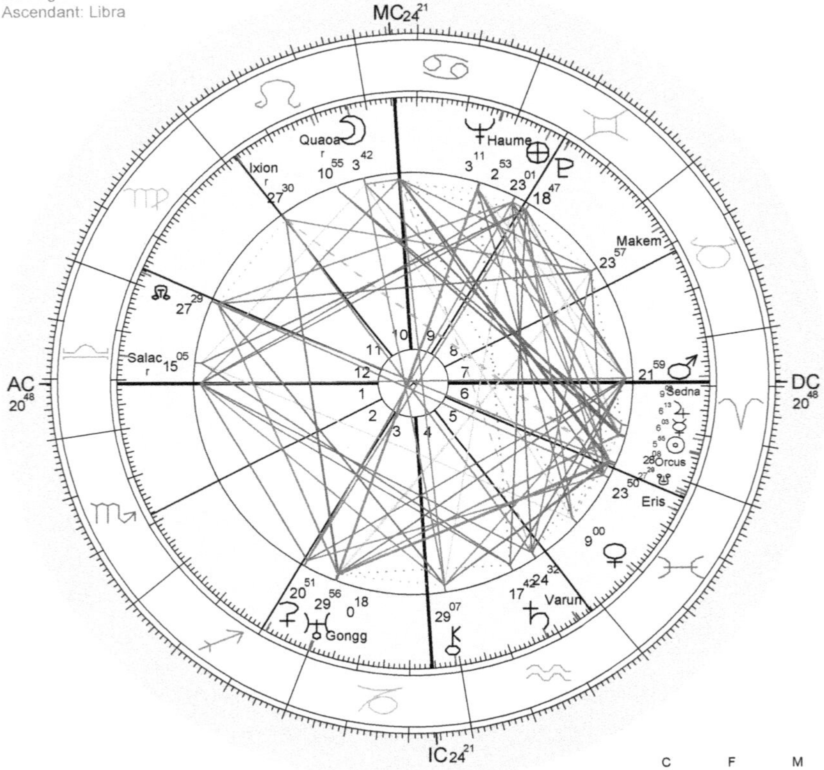

	C	F	M
F	☉☿♂♃Se	☽ IxQu	♅ ⚳
A	SaAC	♄Va	♇ ⊕
E	⚷Go	Ma	☊
W	♆HaMC		♀ ☋ ErOr

☉ Sun	5 Ari	55'22"	
☽ Moon	3 Leo	41'31"	
☿ Mercury	6 Ari	3'17"	
♀ Venus	9 Pis	0'20"	
♂ Mars	21 Ari	59'16"	
♃ Jupiter	8 Ari	12'50"	
♄ Saturn	17 Aqu	42'13"	
♅ Uranus	29 Sag	55'33"	
♆ Neptune	3 Can	10'51"	
♇ Pluto	18 Gem	47' 1"	
☊ True Node	27 Vir	28'40"d	
☋ Desc.T.Node	27 Pis	28'40"d	
⚷ Chiron	29 Cap	7'13"	
⊕ P.Fort.	23 Gem	1'27"	
⚳ Ceres	20 Sag	50'33"	
136108 Haumea	2 Can	52'54"	
136472 Makemake	23 Tau	57' 2"	
225088 Gonggong	0 Cap	17'57"	
120347 Salacia	15 Lib	5'23"r	
136199 Eris	23 Pis	49'41"	
28978 Ixion	27 Leo	29'58"r	
90482 Orcus	28 Pis	8'19"	
50000 Quaoar	10 Leo	55' 5"r	
90377 Sedna	9 Ari	2'22"	
20000 Varuna	24 Aqu	32' 0"	
AC: 20 Lib 47'37"	2: 18 Sco 21'	3: 19 Sag 59'	
MC: 24 Can 21'14"	11: 27 Leo 40'	12: 26 Vir 44'	

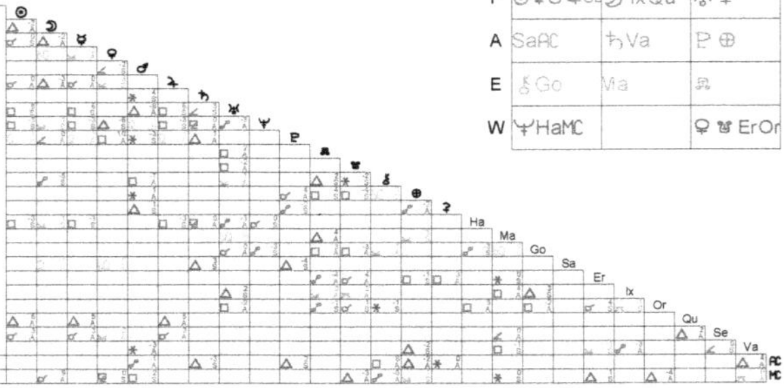

- *The Mystical/Metaphysical Function - Awakening and maintaining in the individual a sense of awe and gratitude before the 'mystery of being' and his or her participation in it.*
- *The Cosmological Function - Explaining the shape of the universe.*
- *The Sociological Function - Validating and supporting the existing social order.*
- *The Pedagogical/Psychological Function - Guiding the individual through the stages of life.*[5]

And this conjunction of Haumea and Neptune is in a wide trine to his Venus in the 5th house, so his psychic connection flowed with his values and creativity. One of his most identifiable and most quoted sayings is, "follow your bliss". This has become a mantra for many, providing a helpful guide along the hero's journey that each of us walks through life. Here's how he put it:

> *"If you follow your bliss, you put yourself on a kind of track that has been there all the while, waiting for you, and the life that you ought to be living is the one you are living. Wherever you are – if you are following your bliss, you are enjoying that refreshment, that life within you, all the time."*[6]

His Haumea/Neptune conjunction is opposite Uranus conjunct Gonggong in the 3rd house. And this opposition is in a T-square his close Sun, Mercury, Jupiter, Orcus stellium in the 6th. Sedna joins this conjunction within 6 degrees.

> *"As a strong believer in the psychic unity of mankind and its poetic expression through mythology, he made use of the concept to express the idea*

---

5 https://en.wikipedia.org/wiki/Joseph_Campbell
6 https://jcf.org/about-joseph-campbell/follow-your-bliss/

that the whole of the human race can be seen as engaged in the effort of making the world "transparent to transcendence" by showing that underneath the world of phenomena lies an eternal source which is constantly pouring its energies into this world of time, suffering, and ultimately death."[7]

Transit Case Study - Hero with a Thousand Faces

Campbell's seminal book, *Hero with a Thousand Faces,* was published on 1 January 1949. In this he looked at myths across cultures and discovered an archetypal mythology that underlies all myths. He saw this through his Neptune conjunct Haumea in the 9th house and realized that essentially, we are all one.

On the day of the publication transiting Haumea was sesquiquadrate his natal Mercury/Sun/Jupiter conjunction in the 6th house, referencing the work he's doing in his daily rhythm to birth this new understanding.

Haumea was transiting through his 10th house, encouraging a rebirth in his social role and was also sextile his Ascendant, and therefore flowing with his self-expression. She was also in a close trine with his natal Ceres in the 3rd house. Ceres represents a give and take of love, and she was on the cusp of the 3rd house of ideas, which indicates that he launched his book with love and pastoral care. And we certainly see this in its reception.

Meanwhile transiting North Node in the 7th house was closely sextile his natal conjunction of Haumea and Neptune. This means his practical destiny in the one-to-one house of engaging with people was supporting the successful launch of his book. As we know from this vantage point in history, he fulfilled this destiny.

---

7   https://en.wikipedia.org/wiki/Joseph_Campbell

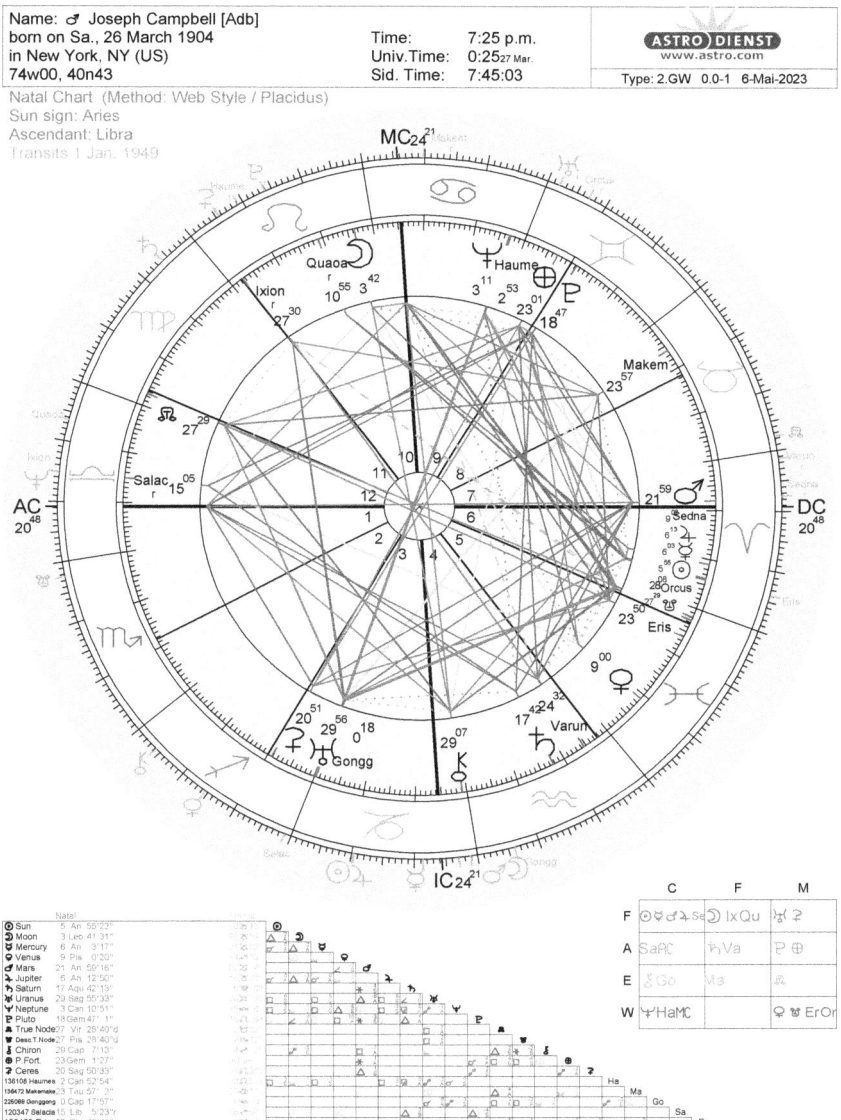

Haumea in the Signs

Haumea in Leo

Those born after 1927 and before 1960 have Haumea in Leo. Nurturing our spirit and growing through that process is very important to those of us with this placement. We value spirituality and equate growth with spiritual growth.

With this placement we have been validating this spiritual centering and championing that for the rest of society. We pioneered what is now becoming mainstream. We are taking the individual relationship to spirit out of the hands of an external authority.

Haumea has volcanic power so she can represent a violent rebirth where everything is transformed in an instant and those of us born with it in the proud fire sign of Leo need to channel that potentially explosive power constructively.

If we are born in the latter half of that time, from 1945 to 1960, we have a Pluto/Haumea conjunction. When we have a conjunction, but only know one of the planets, we attribute both meanings to one we know is there. So, while traditionally Pluto is seen as representing both death and rebirth, in our emerging solar system he is more about the death which makes space for Haumea's renewal.

Haumea breathes spiritual renewal into our lives, connecting us to the psychic center and enabling an evolution in our spiritual consciousness. And those born with this conjunction have a unique role to play in birthing our new psychic unity.

Haumea in Virgo

If we are born between 1960 and 1993, we have Haumea in Virgo. This placement brings out the earth goddess side of Haumea, rather than the fire goddess. So, with this placement we tend to be calm and peaceful, seeking a natural harmony and ongoing rejuvenation in all aspects of our lives if the planet is well-placed. Or, if it is not well-placed, we can struggle with allowing that regeneration.

We understand that there is an ecology within us that we need to nurture and that this is echoed in our outer ecology. We often don't recognize the link between the inner and outer ecologies, which can lead us to be violent to others without realizing that this is reflected in our inner psyche.

Those of us with this placement have an ecological awareness and environmental activism that didn't exist before. We have a recognition of how everything is interconnected, and this gives us the power to change our impact.

Changing family structures has also been a focus for those of us with Haumea in Virgo. We are moving from the nuclear family to a wider understanding of what family is. Alienation from our environment has created a desire to belong, and we are seeking conscious community that is larger than blood ties.

We want to birth in a more organic, ecstatic way than the traditional medical system allows. Our approach to birthing is not locked into medical intervention but allows for the transformation of pain to pleasure. We embrace the radical view that birth is the natural result of sex and is therefore a sexual act.

Haumea in Libra

At the end of 2022 Haumea went into Scorpio, so those of us born after 1993 have Haumea in Libra. This is a sign that seeks to rebalance the relationships between people, nations, religions, and the earth. So, with this placement we will bring a never-ending source of energy to this balancing process and will continuously strive for the welfare of ourselves and our loved ones.

We have a natural sense of justice that seeks to transcend cultural differences across society. An urge to right the wrongs. We are not trying to make everyone the same but rather to honor the variety by mediating injustices which come from prejudices such as sexism, ableism, or racism.

With Haumea going into Libra, we have evolved a new creative activist form called artivism, where we use art to communicate social injustices. Those of us with this placement will be particularly drawn to creative new ways to come together and express ourselves. Through our work there will likely be a cross-fertilization of previously discrete realms of expression.

With this placement we are very creative and with the technology available to us these days we don't have to be DaVinci to create a wonderful artwork. With Haumea in this sign, if we work creatively, we will be renaissance artists, recreating artistic expression by bringing traditional art into new forms.

As we tune-in to our more spiritual nature, there may be a temporary imbalance as we adjust to the ramifications of establishing new values. We can then access a psychic strength to challenge existing ideas and values to understand our life in a new way.

Haumea in the Houses

1st House

Haumea represents a psychic connection and in the first house this is to the center of ourselves. Planets in this house influence our personality and with Haumea here the 'magic of being' infuses our body and our views on life with a rich creative energy.

At the personal planet level of consciousness however this can manifest as an extremely egocentric approach. And because this house is about how others perceive us, we may come across as very self-involved.

As we adopt a more spiritual approach, however, we can develop a willful self-awareness which mitigates this, together with a rock-solid integrity that others can feel.

Hans Christian Anderson is an example. His magic of being inspired numerous generations. His fables of morality were translated into more than a hundred languages, more than any book other than the Bible. And, exemplifying the self-involvement of this house, he also wrote three autobiographies.

When we're on the spiritual path this placement nourishes our adaptability and resourcefulness with the life-giving properties of Haumea. As we deepen our contact with Source, we can develop a soulful confidence and may have the ability to foster psychic unity.

Like New Zealander Faye Blake-Cossar, who runs an astrology school in Amsterdam. Her master's dissertation offers a *life cycle model for organizational development* and her work focuses on making clients feel safe while applying her extensive training in Inner Child Integration Therapy.

2nd house

With Haumea in the second house, we may be able to bring about a material rejuvenation, both in our own lives and in the world around us.

At the personal planet consciousness level, we may have a bit of a bulldozer approach to our security needs and to our sensual pleasures, which may be successful in the short term, but things like bullying are not sustainable practices for a healthy life, nor is relying on non-paid volunteers, fans, or devotees for support. With this placement we need to ensure that we are giving as much as we are receiving on both the material and the psychic levels and that we remain faithful to our values.

As we develop a more spiritual approach, we likely have a deep appreciation of our sensual experience and of nature, and we understand the humanizing and social function of art.

Because the second house is about cultivation and Haumea is about fostering and fertility this is a very creative and generative placement.

Like Mae West, who wrote most of her material and became an icon of sexual power and femininity. She was so faithful to her values of free creative and sexual expression that she was prosecuted for moral charges because her first Broadway play, *Sex*, depicted homosexuality. She bailed her cast out, but she chose to stay in jail herself to garner the publicity. We see the generative power of Haumea in this house in her status as the 2nd highest paid person in the U.S. at the height of her career.

As we deepen our contact with Source, this can bring a bountiful process of renewal of wealth and material possessions into our lives and our sense of self-worth can also enjoy a constant state of renewal.

We see this in the Dalai Lama, who through his faithfulness to his values, and despite huge material challenges, has been able to draw support and finance to the Tibetan cause for freedom, which has enabled a renewal of Buddhism internationally.

3rd House

The renewal in the third house is in our ideas, our communications, and our immediate environment. Haumea is always searching for spiritual answers and in this house that curiosity infuses all our communications if we can see the forest for the trees.

At the personal planet level, because this house talks about the lower mind, we may get lost in the trees, lost in the detail, and feel insecure in these contacts. And we may make up for this by demanding attention, or by making claims of martyrdom and sacrifice to secure attention.

As we develop a more spiritual approach there is likely a renewal process occurring in our thinking patterns which keeps them fresh and relevant and gives us the insight to see the divinity of human beings and the oneness of existence.

Like Erica Jong who wrote *Fear of Flying*, which became controversial for its depiction of female sexuality. Her work catalyzed the development of second-wave feminism. Along with her contribution to intellectual renewal, she was married four times, embodying Haumea's ability to be reborn.

Or like musician Van Morrison, who Rolling Stone magazine commented had *"the striking imagination of a consciousness that is visionary in the strongest sense of the word"*.[8] He describes himself as a Christian Mystic and has investigated various religions, which serve as inspiration for his music.

As we deepen our contact with Source, there can be an unshakeable personal inner knowing, and Haumea's ability to reconstruct, redefine, transform, especially regarding consciousness, is strengthened with this placement.

4th house

This house is the base of our consciousness, it is the sacred ground in which our consciousness is rooted, and with Haumea here we have a psychic connection to the oneness of humanity embedded within that consciousness.

At the personal planet level, however, this house shows the karmic baggage we brought with us into this life. And Haumea's placement here might make us a little too self-centered and a little too invested in getting our way so that we adopt a forceful approach. This house talks about instinctive behavior and Haumea is about opening doors within us, so our level of consciousness is crucial in seeing and evaluating those doors.

Author Salman Rushdie has this placement. His work primarily deals with connections, disruptions, and migrations. His book *The Satanic Verses* generated a debate in the Muslim world, which provoked a renewal in the religion, together with a backlash. As a result, for many years he was confined in the sacred space of his 4th house for his own safety.

As we develop a more spiritual approach, we can bring the spiritual wealth and rejuvenation of Haumea into our home and our inner emotional security. For those who believe in reincarnation, the 4th house gives us clues to our karmic

---

[8] https://www.rollingstone.com/music/music-news/van-morrison-to-revisit-moondance-with-reissue-72914/

lesson for this lifetime and with Haumea here the lesson is to reconnect with the psychic unity of humanity across time and space, to feel the oneness of existence.

Margaret Atwood has this placement. Her written works encompass themes such as gender and identity, religion and myth, the power of language, and climate change. Her famous sci-fi book, *The Handmaid's Tale,* explores the interdependence of the sexes in a futuristic dystopian world, causing the reader to question the usury nature of our relationships and move beyond them into embodying psychic unity.

As we deepen our contact with Source, the base of consciousness symbolized by the 4th house becomes a fertile sacred ground nourishing our higher consciousness.

5th house

The 5th house is all about us being ourselves and enjoying it, and with Haumea here we will likely be very creative in this process and our joy will have a regenerative effect on ourselves and others.

At the personal planet level of consciousness however we may come on too strong in our love affairs, our creative self-expression, and our parenting. There is a risk of being overly dramatic and attention seeking as a cover for our lack of real psychic connection. And this is the house of risk-taking, so we must be careful not to fill any lack of connection with others with hollow pleasures like gambling.

As we develop a more spiritual approach, we can learn to bring a spirit of play into our romantic affairs, our creativity, and our parenting, and to take the risks necessary to grow in these areas.

Like Philip K. Dick, whose fiction explored philosophical and social questions such as the nature of reality, perception, human nature, and identity. He was married 5 times. Later in his life, following a series of mystical experiences, his work moved into the realms of theology and metaphysics.

And as we deepen our contact with Source, we gain a passionate understanding of the humanizing and social functions of art. At this level the fostering ability and fertility of Haumea gives us a rich bounty of joy and love as the creative medium of our work.

Centering in love, Elisabeth Kubler-Ross, Swiss psychiatrist and author, is noted for her work in renewing our relationship to dying and death. Her belief in the continuity of life spirit through the experience of death enabled her to assist more than 20,000 people with their passage into an afterlife.

6th House

With Haumea in the house of routine tasks and duties, every moment can be alive with spirit and in touch with the magic of being.

At the personal planet level of consciousness, however, we may not be aware of this and worry about our lack of meaningful connection could manifest in our lives as anxiety disorders. We have to be mindful not to play the hypochondriac or be attention seeking to compensate.

This house also talks about our method of responding to everyday crises and at this level we may ride roughshod over people because of the urgency of our immediate demand. As we develop a more spiritual approach, Haumea gives us the willfulness to seek a strong psychic connection in each moment and the regenerative strength required in moments of crisis.

We see this in Farida, Queen of Egypt, who liberated women in Egyptian culture from their secluded role as mothers to participants in society. She did this by taking a public role as queen in her marriage, which also freed the other royal women from the seclusion of the harem. She later gave up the status of queen in order to divorce her husband and gain her personal freedom.

As we deepen our contact with Source, Haumea gives us the courage to see the divinity of human beings and the oneness of existence in every moment. At this level we have an ability to reach out into the psychic soil around us and connect with both a larger wisdom and an unshakeable personal inner knowing.

Like Reinhold Ebertin, considered the founder of Cosmobiology. This holds that cosmic energies influence biological processes on Earth. This influence is evidenced by the Moon's impact on our waters. His work in this branch of astrology integrates psychology, medicine, sociology, and biology into an understanding of the rhythms of our daily lives.

7th house

This is the house of one-to-one relationships and with Haumea here our search for spirit is answered through our relationships. Seventh house relationships are about cooperation and sharing, and they generally serve some functional purpose in the larger social community.

At the personal planet level of consciousness, however, we may experience quarrels and separation in our relationships if we are not tuning in to our partner. The lack of respect implied by our insensitivity can breed open enemies and lawsuits.

American filmmaker Francis Ford Coppola had a rollercoaster career which forced him into bankruptcy three times in ten years as a result of bad investments of his early film profits. His iconic movie "The Godfather" nevertheless had a defining effect on modern culture. He was initially reluctant to direct it until he focused on the deeper themes of family and capitalism in America.

As we develop a more spiritual approach, we can engage in diplomacy which opens doors for us and others. Haumea's renewal comes both through a reconnection with our inner fountain of youth and with the collective psyche through our one-to-one relationships.

Like Jane Fonda, who has undergone a variety of reinventions in her life. These include actor, exercise guru, feminist, political activist, author, businesswoman, and wife to a number of famous men. The title of her autobiography encapsulates this: *Prime Time: Love, Health, Sex, Fitness, Friendship, Spirit – making the most of all of your life.*

As we deepen our contact with Source, we can reach a state of psychic equilibrium and enjoy rock solid integrity in our contracts and all official matters.

8th house

This House rules those processes and things by which we transform and become more powerful, including through sexual interaction.

At the personal planet level of consciousness, transformation usually requires some type of death, loss, or injury first. This is the house of karma, where we make personal sacrifices for the collective and at this level, we may be a bit of a drama queen about this, because Haumea likes to make claims of martyrdom and sacrifice to secure attention. Or we could abuse our psychic sensitivity by using other people's energy, by taking advantage of non-paid volunteers, fans, or devotees.

However, as we develop a more spiritual approach, the regenerative nature of both the house and the planet work together to allow a flowing spring of spirit into our lives, keeping us in touch with the magic of being.

Like Masaru Emoto, original thinker, Japanese artist, and author of *The Hidden Messages in Water*. His extensive research and photography of the frozen crystal form of water gave humanity striking visuals of how water is affected at a molecular level by what's around it.

Or like Jane Goodall, who is the world's leading expert in the family and social life of chimpanzees. She observed behaviors that we consider only human, like hugging, kissing, and even tickling, saying that *"it isn't only human beings who have personality, who are capable of rational thought and emotions like joy and sorrow."*[9] In later years she founded Roots & Shoots, which brings together youth worldwide to work on environmental conservation and humanitarian issues.

As we deepen our contact with Source, we strengthen our occult ability, understanding the give and take required to maintain this flow. At this level, our sensitivity to the collective psychic energies can bring the clairvoyance to see how these will play out.

9th House

Haumea is always searching for spiritual answers, and in the 9th house this is about the experiences we encounter when we search for the meaning of things.

At the personal planet level of consciousness, we could be locked into belief systems and experience head-on collisions with others who believe differently. Or we could feel insecure in these areas, unable to make enough spiritual connection to make any sense out of our experience.

However, Haumea has an ability to reconstruct, redefine and transform, especially regarding consciousness. And as we develop a more spiritual approach this is about understanding, which involves synthesizing known data, so we discover larger fields of social existence.

---

9 https://www.janegoodall.org.nz/africa-programmes/research/

Like Patch Adams, who maintains that humor and joy are more important than any drug or therapy in the healing process. Recovering from psychological problems himself, he went back to school to become a doctor and set up the Gesundheit Institute, where he charges no fees, has no malpractice insurance, and lives with his patients in a country farm setting. At the institute medicine is integrated with the performing arts, arts and crafts, agriculture, nature, recreation, and social service.

As we deepen our contact with Source, this placement can bring an unshakeable personal inner knowing and put us in touch with the magic of being, accentuating Haumea's profound idealism and sense of freedom as the highest principle.

We see this in Icelandic musician Bjork's political support of liberation movements for Kosovo and Greenland. She also supports the individuality of young artists by helping them launch their careers. Her music is unique, and she and her fans share an alternative view of the universe. *"I think there's a spiritual element in everything. Walking down the street can be spiritual or it can be silly. It's up to the person. I can definitely say that making and listening to music are spiritual experiences for me."*[10]

10th House

This house encompasses the most public areas of our lives and the career that we develop, and with Haumea here we are in tune with society and are likely to be a reformer.

At the personal planet level of consciousness, however, we may have trouble connecting with this psychic oneness of society and so may come on too strong with our answer for others, alienating them and making our job harder.

---

10 https://www.innerviews.org/inner/bjork.html

But as we develop a more spiritual approach, we can open ourselves to this oneness that is all around us and draw strength from this, understanding the bigger picture. This house includes the social foundations of recognition for achievements and sense of duty to society. Haumea's placement here can bring the insight to see the divinity of human beings in all these activities.

Like Scottish observational comedian Billy Connolly, known for his crass use of language and reference to human bodily functions. This irreverence dissolves the social boundaries, uniting us as humans. *"I think it's time for people to get together, not split apart. The more people stay together, the happier they'll be."* [11]

As we deepen our contact with Source, we can embody this divinity and develop the spiritual wealth and rock-solid integrity that is the basis of the community power and prestige of this house.

Like Italian educator Maria Montessori, who developed The Montessori Method which emphasizes the development of a child's own initiative and natural abilities, through practical play. This method provided educators with a new understanding of child development that allows children to develop at their own pace.

11th House

The psychic connection with Haumea in the 11th house is to our community, to the collective consciousness.

At the personal planet level of consciousness, however, this can manifest as a lack of connection, because our sense of belonging is inward-looking. Or we may seek indiscriminate connection with friends or groups, or force a connection,

---

11 https://en.wikipedia.org/wiki/Billy_Connolly

because we are so desperate for belonging that we do not evaluate friends or groups appropriately.

As we develop a more spiritual approach however, we can become more sensitive to this process and more aware of consciousness. At this level the collective consciousness provides a rich field of opportunity for the profound idealism of Haumea, and we will actively seek out groups with like-minded views.

Leading Mexican artist Frida Kahlo exemplifies this profound idealism: *"I have a great restlessness about my paintings. Mainly because I want to make it useful to the revolutionary communist movement...until now I have managed simply an honest expression of my own self..."*[12] Today she is regarded as an icon for the feminism movement, the LGBTQ+ community, and for Chicanos, the culture which embodies the in-between nature of cultural hybridity that is neither fully American nor Mexican.

As we deepen our contact with Source, the love and charity of this house combines with the spiritual wealth of Haumea, to enable us to redefine and transform the collective consciousness and foster the 'magic of being' in our lives and the lives of those around us.

Like Leonard Cohen, whose spirituality permeated all his work. He evolved from struggling writer to successful singer and songwriter and then became a Zen monk. Through his music we shared in his personal spiritual journey from an alienated space as a younger person to a strong connection with the magic of being alive. His music is known for being bittersweet yet gracefully expressing the dark night of the soul.

---

[12] https://en.wikipedia.org/wiki/Frida_Kahlo

12th House

This is the house of the collective unconscious and of spiritual realization and Haumea's placement here gives the potential for deep spiritual connection. It is also the house of the subconscious, which is the hidden self that exists apart from our physical everyday reality. So, at the personal planet level of consciousness, we may not be in touch with this side of ourselves. As a result, we may inadvertently expose ourselves or have issues of privacy.

Finding refuge, seclusion, or retreat may help us to reconnect with our inner magic of being.

This is the house of spiritual realization and Haumea is spiritual wealth. As we adopt a more spiritual approach, we can develop a psychic connection to the unconscious and over time this will enable luck and miracles in our life.

Like musician Arlo Guthrie, who bought an old church and made it into a charitable center that serves people of all religions. He does this through free lunches, aid for family farmers, and services for abused children and the elderly. As a renowned folk singer-songwriter he also holds a number of fundraising concerts each year that support families living with life-threatening illnesses. His personal exploration of spirituality includes Catholicism, Judaism, and Hinduism.

As we deepen our contact with Source, the supportive, fostering energies of Haumea combine with the healing, forgiveness, and peacefulness of this house to allow a deep spiritual connection with the oneness of existence.

Like Annie Besant who was deeply religious as a child and longed to serve humanity. Which she did as president of the Theosophical Society for 25 years. In that role she fostered the young Krishnamurti, through her World Teacher Project, as the new spiritual avatar. She had a great love of ritual and ceremony and wrote more than 300 books and pamphlets.

Workbook to Onboard Haumea in Your Life

1. Work out where Haumea is in your birth chart:
   a. Go to www.astro.com and create a free account.
   b. Then choose "Extended Chart Selection" under "Charts & Data" and put in your birth data.
   c. On this data screen, at the bottom on the left under 'Additional Objects', you can choose to include the dwarfs, which are listed as Asteroids, and you do this by highlighting them. The dwarfs in this box are *Ceres, Eris, Ixion, Orcus, Quaoar, Sedna & Varuna.*
   d. Then opposite this, in the box on the bottom right, add these numbers (**136108,136472, 225088, 120347**) to also include *Haumea, Makemake, Gonggong & Salacia.*
   e. Click 'Show the Chart' to see it.
   f. Then click 'Additional Tables' at the top left of the chart to get the table of positions and aspects.
2. Look up the house interpretation in this book for your house placement and see what resonates.
3. What does the Sabian Symbol for your Haumea indicate to you? Search online for Dane Rudhyar's or

Marc Edmund Jones's interpretations. (Remember to round up to find the right symbol, i.e. 22.04 = 23).

4. Next, understand how Haumea interacts with the other planets in your chart by studying the aspects. I.e. – is Haumea conjunct, opposite, trine, square or sextile any of your personal planets or points like Sun, Moon, Ascendant, Mercury, Venus, Ceres, Mars, Jupiter, or Saturn? How about the transpersonal planets like Uranus, Neptune, Pluto, Ixion, Orcus, Salacia, Quaoar, Makemake, Gonggong, Eris and Sedna?

5. Choose a significant moment of rebirth in your life and look up the transits of Pluto and Saturn to your natal Haumea on that date. You can find the list of where these two planets on this ephemeris: https://www.astro.com/swisseph/swepha_e.htm. And then check the Haumea transits to your other natal planet. You can find the Haumea ephemeris at this link: https://www.astro.com/swisseph/haumea.htm.

6. Given what you've learned so far, write a couple of paragraphs on how you can best activate Haumea in your life.

Haumea's Place in our New Firmament

The outer planets represent aspects of consciousness. We have become familiar with Uranus, Neptune and Pluto, and over the early years of this century we have discovered 10 new planets who offer us a rich feast of new consciousness. Let's look at each of these outer planets to put them in context.

As we embark on the spiritual path to make a larger sense out of the experiences of our personal lives, we start activating our Uranian and Neptunian energies and bring them into our consciousness. As we do, we begin to realize that the 'you can't take it with you' approach of the inner planets is actually a delusion.

Uranus brings intuitive flashes into our personal planet consciousness and begins to connect us with the collective consciousness, breaking through our Saturnian defenses to allow new impulses and connections. So, the discovery of Uranus enabled consciousness growth in our lives. We can look at Uranus as the higher octave of Mercury because he takes Mercury's ideas, communications and curiosity, and networks them at a higher spiritual level.

Neptune tunes us into the bigger picture and brings spiritual consciousness into our lives. He encourages us to search for a larger meaning for our personal experiences and teaches us about faith as a way of deepening consciousness. Neptune is traditionally considered to be the higher octave of Venus, where the inner planet's values and aesthetics are expressed at a more spiritual level through the imagination and psychic opening of Neptune.

Which brings us to dwarf planet **Pluto**, who is the start of the outer transpersonal planets. Here we must accept the limitations of the ego consciousness, let go of compulsions and unconscious constructs and accept that change is the only constant. Pluto is traditionally considered to be the higher octave of Mars.

The discovery of Pluto enabled the psychological understanding of our lives. This produced the shadow paradigm, where the darkness in our souls is seen to be buried in our unconscious, and the convenience of this is that we don't have to address it on a day-to-day basis. But we need to ditch Pluto's shadow paradigm to enable him and these other new energies consciously in our lives. As with all the other outer planets, Pluto manifests differently depending on our level of consciousness, so what we have been calling his shadow is simply his manifestation when we are at personal planet consciousness.

As we get on the spiritual path, Pluto gives us an adaptability and resilience which enables us to mediate the transition occurring in our lives in each moment. And at the spiritually evolved level, we can transmute loneliness and separation into love and long-term relationships and effect a regeneration in our lives.

Pluto now has two new brothers who share his orbit and his angle to the ecliptic. They also share his gravitational resonance with Neptune, as all three do two orbits of the Sun, to every three of Neptune's. However, these brothers are polar opposites.

The first is **Ixion**, who encourages us to be a passionate, but lawless, follower of our heart, or loins, depending on our consciousness level. He's always asking the question: 'are the rules we're playing by the right ones?' And he does this by pushing the boundaries and asking for forgiveness afterwards, rather than permission before. As we develop a spiritual approach, we can learn to honor the bad girl or bad boy energy inside us and follow our heart. At this level Ixion encourages us to be an independent and unique expression of ourselves, while being sensitive to the unspoken agreements in our relationships, so we know how far we can go.

The second is Pluto's straight-talking brother, **Orcus**. He is the master of integrity at the highest level, but he also encourages us to engage in double-talk and deception at the personal planet level. As we develop spiritually however, he gives us a self-sufficiency that will nourish us through the long and difficult work that we sometimes find necessary, plus a capacity to deal with the shadow side of our lives. At this level we become accountable for our deeds and actions. We learn to align with a spiritual creed and understand the karmic process of life. And, at the highest level, we gain the shamanic ability to transmute shadow into light.

Just beyond Orcus, we have **Salacia**, who gives us a self-protective quality that helps us weather the real and psychic storms. She can give us the power to foresee opportunities and find the appropriate time to embrace them. She enables us to take a leap of faith, especially when we know we are going to be profoundly transformed by the experience. At the personal planet level there can be erotic fascination or interest, and socially unacceptable, often illicit, sexual activity. And in challenging or difficult aspect, we might feel not in control or unable to change a situation. At the highest level, however, Salacia is about bringing true love into our lives and empowering us spiritually.

Next, we have **Varuna**, who is the higher octave of Saturn. Where Saturn rules by control and through laws and restriction, Varuna has a natural sovereignty, but we have to claim this through action. Sovereignty is a dance between our intention and the collective psyche. We have to claim it and at the same time others have to agree to give it to us. We start this process by stepping forth in some way and saying 'I can do this'. And then we have to keep doing it over time. And, when we do, we gain support and notability for this work. Once we are on the spiritual path, Varuna teaches us to stand in the center of our lives and own the results of our dance of karma and dharma.

As we move further out from the Sun, we find **Haumea**, who is a creation deity of the Hawaiian people. She is both an earth goddess and a fire goddess, and she represents regeneration and rebirth. She is the higher octave of Neptune, turning his psychic opening into real psychic connection. At the personal planet level however, this can manifest as a lack of connection, a sort of spiritual alienation. As we develop spiritually, she provides a link with the oneness of humanity, with the magic of being alive. So, she represents a direct link with the soul level when we can open ourselves to it.

Next, we have our first non-gendered planet, **Quaoar**, the creation deity of the Tongva people, who are indigenous to Los Angeles. Quaoar sings and dances the world into existence, so this planet talks about a practice of bringing spirit into matter. Singing and dancing are practices that bring spirit into matter, and so are yoga, meditation, walking in the woods, and many other things. Anything can be a practice to bring spirit into our lives. We can look at Quaoar as the higher octave of Jupiter. Where Jupiter is a sort of dumb luck, Quaoar turns each moment into a dynamic meditation where we can see the opportunities and act on them in real time, so Quaoar is like smart luck.

Our next planet is **Makemake**, who is the higher octave of Uranus. Makemake takes Uranus's intuitive network and talks about the rich context that it addresses, about the culture, or the nation that is created as a result. At the personal planet level, we might use this rich intuitive understanding to hide in plain sight, to blend into the background as a safety mechanism. As we develop spiritually, however, he calls spiritual nourishment into our lives and gives us a devotional focus bordering on genius.

This is followed by **Gonggong**, who is a Chinese water god. He is an empathic wizard at the highest level, able to feel inside other people and walk a mile in their shoes. We have to get out of our own emotions to empathize with others however, so at the personal planet level, he can be a bit of an enfant terrible, encouraging us to be very emotionally self-indulgent and to lash out in an attempt to get our own way. As we develop spiritually, we can lift our energy out of our personal space and empathize with others. Empathy allows us to motivate others from the inside, to combine our energies and lift the spiritual vibe.

Then we have **Eris**, who is the warrior sister of Mars in myth. And we know that Pluto is the higher octave of Mars, so Eris is the higher octave of Pluto. She shines her fierce grace on everything in our lives, seeking inclusion and validation for all the disparate facets of our psyche. At the personal planet level, she encourages us to engage in discord and strife, so we learn to stop fooling ourselves, or stop being fooled. But as we adopt a more spiritual approach, she enables us to see clearly without preconceptions and keep our body and mind in harmony so that health and happiness prevails. And at the top level she is a spirit-guide, transmuting life into love.

And finally, we have the new outer limit of our solar system, **Sedna**, who is always trying to get us onto the spiritual path. She represents *Our Soul's Path of Destiny* because, if we accept that our soul incarnates over a number of lifetimes and that it has a purpose to grow through these incarnations, then in this life, that purpose is shown by the Sedna placement.

We can think of Sedna as the higher octave of **Ceres**, who is our newly reclassified inner dwarf planet, orbiting between Mars and Jupiter. Ceres is our ability to love and be loved. At both a basic level and in the bigger sense of the word, she represents what we need to feed and nourish ourselves. We can think of Ceres as the higher octave of the Moon. The Moon is our emotional center, the other luminary in our chart, where we see ourselves reflected in each moment. The Moon mediates our survival through each of those moments and Ceres talks of the process of those moments and mediates our survival over time.

Sedna steps this heart-centered energy all the way out to the new limit of our solar system, so she speaks to our survival over lifetimes. Here we learn to let go of the physical realm and allow transcendence to a new wholistic spiritual consciousness where we can allow love and harmony, and nurture abundance.

Dwarf Planets as Higher Octaves

Here is a framework of higher octaves to help us understand several of the dwarf planets. A higher octave expresses an inner planet energy at a more spiritual level. But as Dane Rudhyar reminds us in the below quote from Horoscope Magazine, the higher octaves act on the lower octaves to repolarize and transform them. (The planets in bold are dwarf planets).

Sedna - **Ceres** - Moon

Haumea – Neptune – Venus

Makemake – Uranus – Mercury

Eris – **Pluto** – Mars

Quaoar – Jupiter

Varuna - Saturn

When Uranus, Neptune and Pluto are considered as "higher" expressions of such planets as Mercury, Venus and Mars… the closer planets are seen to represent a "lower octave" of biological-personal functions or energies; the more remote ones, beyond Saturn, a "higher octave" constituted of more transcendent and "spiritual" activities or qualities of being.

There is some truth, no doubt, in such statements if one restricts oneself to a consideration of only the external events of a person's life. The "illuminations" which Uranus may bring to the consciousness that is not frozen into Saturnian rigidity can inspire and transform the Mercury mind. The compassion and inclusiveness which are characteristic of Neptune do act directly — if allowed by Saturn so to act—upon the sense of value and the feeling-judgments represented by Venus. The power of inescapable destiny and total surrender to a cause, which defines essentially Pluto's operations, do transform — if allowed to do so — the strictly personal initiative of Mars.

But the essential fact is that the activities of Uranus, Neptune and Pluto run counter to the normal functions of Mercury, Venus and Mars. The former are not just personal activities of a "higher" kind; they are activities meant to disturb and transform — indeed, utterly to repolarize and reorient those of Mercury, Venus and Mars.[13]

---

13 https://www.khaldea.com/rudhyar/astroarticles/planetaryoctaves.php

Dwarf Planet University

The information in this book comes out of research at the Dwarf Planet University, where we are pioneering the astrological exploration of the Kuiper Belt. The dwarf planets speak of new aspects of consciousness that are arising in our lives, and we offer 6-week courses to on-board each of them.

The courses explore the planets in our personal chart and the charts of the other class members. We study the house placement, the aspects, and research our transits, as we understand how to on-board each aspect of consciousness.

The course format mixes webinars, blog-posted assignments, and live Zoom Q&As, so you can attend from anywhere in the world. We start with a live Welcome Q&A, and we explore the House position in the first fortnight, the aspects in the second and transits in the third. Each fortnight includes an instructional webinar, an investigative assignment based on our personal chart and a live 2 hour Zoom Q&A session.

Assignments are posted on a private forum so we can learn from, and comment on, posts from our fellow course members. And the live Q&A sessions are recorded so we can pick up classes we miss.

The students on our courses range from beginners to very experienced astrologers, and it is this range that is the source of the vibrant class culture. What students love is the community sharing that occurs, through the blog-posted assignments and live Zoom Q&As, which gives a good picture of how these new planets act similarly, and yet diversely, in each of our lives.

We offer a Dwarf Planet Astrology Diploma on completion of any 8 of our 11 courses, but you are also welcome to do courses singly and in any order, and all the courses have a mix of ongoing and casual students.

Community Program

We also offer a Community Program which is designed for those who want to explore these new aspects of consciousness, but don't want to commit to assignments and in-depth study.

As a community participant you get a copy of your chart including the dwarfs, and also get access to all 11 on-demand webinars which introduce each dwarf planet. These include the house interpretations, which is where we see these outer planets manifesting most clearly in our lives. These webinars are posted throughout the year, just prior to the start of each course.

You also have the opportunity to participate in four Zoom gatherings throughout the year where Uni founder, Alan Clay, will talk about the current dwarf transits, answer questions, and look at example charts.

What Students Say:

I highly recommend the Dwarf Planets Course for the insights and the amount of new information and perspective gathered. Alan's teaching inspires one and brings new light and spiritual understanding to charts (certainly to mine). His humor and friendly approach made the seminars very enjoyable yet profound.

Elisabetta Quintiliani, Astrologer - Italy

Alan Clay's sensitive, cutting edge wisdom and the community sharing make the classes on the Dwarf Planets compelling and profound. They are as much an exploration as a revelation. Not only mentally stimulating, they are a deep dive into each of our psyche and growth experience. I love them and am looking forward to more.

Karen La Puma, Astrologer, Counselor, Speaker.

I'm very grateful for Alan Clay's insightfully powerful dwarf planet courses. He offers a supportive and welcoming class environment that encourages learning and processing the deep new consciousness of these planets. I totally recommend engaging into this outer realm of alchemy into our inner self!

Sue Rose Minahan, Evolutionary Post-Modern Astrologer

What Alan Clay has created with the Dwarf Planet University is nothing short of genius. His in-depth knowledge and amazing teaching style are unique and what the astrological world has been waiting for. I'm so enjoying learning about our far-reaching dwarf planets amongst a galaxy of friendly, intelligent student astrologers from all over the universe, logging on at their differing time zones.

Eileen Richardson, UK.

Alan Clay's work has transformed my thinking—about my chart, about my practice—even about astrology itself. Alan is a born teacher. -

Ariel Harper Nave, Canada

I absolutely loved the class! As a first time student of astrology, I can honestly say that aside from Alan (a wonderful teacher and guide), every one of the students in the class was a teacher for me. I learned so much and can't wait for the next class to begin. -

Mary Anne Pitt, USA

Who would have thought that studying the dwarf planets would lead to such an expansive awareness of my soul's journey? For this, I am very grateful. The style and structure of Alan's teaching provide the group with a very warm, safe and informative space in which to learn. I love being part of the group. Thank you, Alan. -

Marian Ryan, Energy Therapist, Author, Teacher, UK

Meet the Writers

New Zealander **Alan Clay** is transpersonal astrologer, specialising in the outer planets, and inspired by the work of Dane Rudhyar. Over the years this has broadened into a study of the new dwarf planets, and today he is one of the Kuiper Belt's astrological pioneers.

Alan worked for many years internationally as a clown and a clown teacher, which he describes as being a big research into people and what makes us human. And he combined this with consulting astrology work to explore the depths or our psyche.

He is well known for his clown textbook, *Angels Can Fly*, which includes a mix of clown theory, workshop and street exercises, anecdotes from 20 international clowns, and fictional stories following the adventures of 10 street clowns.

He is also the writer and director of an award winning romantic comedy film, *Courting Chaos*, in which a Beverly Hills girl falls for a Venice Beach street clown called Chaos, and she must overcome her inhibitions and become a clown herself for the relationship to survive.

His book, *Sedna Consciousness, the Soul's Path of Destiny* was launched at UAC 2018 in Chicago. It is the ultimate reference on the new outer limit of our solar system, the planet Sedna. The book includes aspect interpretations with all the traditional planets, as well as all the new dwarf planets.

Following several years of teaching dwarf planet astrology courses online, Alan founded the Dwarf Planet University under the Jupiter/Saturn conjunction in 2000. Since then he has developed all the course material that is used by students at the Uni, and he leads the fortnightly live Zoom Q&As. He still works as a consulting astrologer and is available for chart readings by Zoom.

Melissa Elvira Billington is the child of a healer and a physicist, conceived in a conscientious objector's community in Nova Scotia but born in Virginia and raised in the Northeastern US. She worked in the arts in Santa Fe, Boise, and New York City before heading to India in 1999 for the last full solar eclipse of the last millennium.

As the stars would have it, she has lived and worked as an artist and yoga teacher in India, Barbados, Puerto Rico, New Zealand, and now Australia. She has studied dwarf planet astrology with Alan for five years and worked as an assistant teacher at the Dwarf Planet Uni for the last two.

Here is her first spiritual work, age 7, fresh from the ashram:

Inner and Outer space

is a wondrous place

to be at peace with yourself.

Love is the peace of mind

that binds us together

in outer and inner space as one.

www.ingramcontent.com/pod-product-compliance
Lightning Source LLC
Chambersburg PA
CBHW040054100426
42734CB00043B/3276